QUINCY JONES

—African-American Biographies—

QUINCY JONES

Musician, Composer, Producer

Series Consultant:
Dr. Russell L. Adams, Chairman
Department of Afro-American Studies, Howard University

Lee Hill Kavanaugh

Enslow Publishers, Inc.

44 Fadem Road	PO Box 38
Box 699	Aldershot
Springfield, NJ 07081	Hants GU12 6BP
USA	UK

Library of Congress Cataloging-in-Publication Data

Kavanaugh, Lee Hill.
    Quincy Jones : Musician, composer, producer / Lee Hill
Kavanaugh.
       p. cm. — (African-American biographies)
    Summary: Discusses the life and accomplishments of the jazz
musician, record producer, and composer of movie scores and
television themes.
    Includes bibliographical references (p.) and index.
    ISBN 0-89490-814-6
    1. Jones, Quincy, 1933–   —Juvenile literature. 2. Jazz
musicians—United States—Biography—Juvenile literature.
[1. Jones, Quincy, 1933– . 2. Musicians. 3. Afro-
Americans—Biography.] I. Title. II. Series.
ML3930.J63K38 1997
781.64'092—dc21
    [B]   97-21958
                                                 CIP
                                            AC MN
Printed in the United States of America

10 9 8 7 6 5 4 3 2 1

Illustration Credits: Archive Photos/Darlene Hammond, 65, 79; Archive
Photos/Fotos Int'l, 15, 76, 90, 106; Archive Photos, 84; Archive
Photos/Frank Driggs Collection, 47, 55, 58; Courtesy of Berklee College
of Music Archives, 32; Courtesy of Rutgers University Institute of Jazz
Studies, 41, 44, 68; Reuters/Fred Prouser/Archive Photos, 10; Reuters/Jeff
Christensen/Archive Photos, 100; Reuters/Stringer/Archive Photos, 97.

Cover Illustration: Photo by Harry Benson

CONTENTS

1

DIAL "Q"
FOR SUCCESS

The scenes beaming out of the television news broadcasts across America in November 1984 were not pretty. Ethiopia, a country in eastern Africa, was suffering a famine. Men, women, and children were starving to death. Their faces, witnessed on television, brought their struggles home to America. The images were unforgettable. Something had to be done to help.

On the night of January 28, 1985, in a Los Angeles, California, recording studio, dozens of musical stars gathered to help the best way they knew—with music. The idea was to record a song that would not only awaken the entire world to the famine but also raise thousands (maybe even millions) of dollars to send to Ethiopia.

Forty-five of the world's top musical artists, with different styles ranging from rock 'n' roll to country, arrived at a small studio to record a pop song entitled "We Are the World." Among them were Michael Jackson, Paul Simon, Diana Ross, Bruce Springsteen, Stevie Wonder, Cyndi Lauper, Billy Joel, and Willie Nelson. For ten hours, the musicians blended their voices together first in unison, then in harmony, followed by rests and solos. Every pair of eyes followed the directions of one man—Quincy Jones. It was Jones who stood in front of the crowded studio and conducted their voices as if they were the great horn section of the Count Basie Orchestra.[1] The music, produced by Jones, created magic.

"You could feel the power in the room that night," Jones said. "When you're conducting, it's like forty-five horses—very strong, individualistic, creative people. You could really feel it, and that was a joy. That's something I'll never forget."[2]

The record, conceived by musician Harry Belafonte, became more successful than anyone had dreamed. Within weeks of its release, the six-minute-plus single jumped to the top of the charts. "We Are the World" was the top-selling single of the decade, and it raised $55 million for Ethiopian hunger relief.

"There are very few record producers who would not have been intimidated by that group of people," said country singer Kenny Rogers, who was one of the singers on the recording. "Quincy not only handled it, he handled it delicately, forcefully, tastefully and with tremendous credibility."[3]

As the music producer, Jones had put in weeks of work before the actual recording session. It was Jones who first asked Michael Jackson, the writer of the song along with Lionel Richie, to appear on the record.[4]

It was Jones who wrote letters to all the artists in advance, asking them to "check their egos at the door."[5] This session would not survive if anything other than love were poured into the song, he told them.

It was Jones who planned every detail of the session days before the artists showed up, even deciding which singers would sing solos and determining where each artist would stand so that each voice could be recorded distinctly.[6] There would be no second takes, no second chances.

Years later, Jones still remembers the responsibility as terrifying. With so many megastars, the event could have been a megaflop. No one could predict how the group would work together—these stars had worked only as soloists, never in a choir situation. No one knew what would happen when all these egos came together in one room. With Jones's hard work, the all-night session fell easily into place.

Music producer Quincy Jones was presented with this door sign, "Check Your Egos at the Door," during a party celebrating the tenth anniversary of the "We Are the World" recording. The hit single raised millions of dollars for famine relief in Africa.

"You've just got to do your homework," Jones said. "You can't sit there and decide who's going to sing what on the actual night of the session—that doesn't work with two people let alone forty-five!"[7] Jones's behind-the-scenes touch has turned many songs to gold. Artists in many musical styles—from bebop to hip-hop—have dialed "Q" for success: Sarah Vaughan, Michael Jackson, Ice-T, Frank Sinatra, Nat "King" Cole, Ringo Starr, Aretha Franklin, and Barbra Streisand.

Jones has a gift for dealing with artists on a personal level and bringing out their best musical gifts. "Love and respect force you to pay attention to all the intricacies of those gifts," he explains. "Performers feel this and know you'll never let them get hurt." However, sometimes an artist won't allow Jones to take the lead. Sometimes the artist fears losing control. On those occasions Jones has been known to say: "Let's not get too full of ourselves. Let's leave space for God to come into the room."[8]

Artists respect Jones. His career spans five decades in the music business. From playing trumpet and arranging music for big bands, to composing film scores for dozens of movies and television shows, to producing hundreds of records, Jones has been nominated for an astonishing seventy-seven Grammys (winning twenty-six), along with several Emmy and Oscar nominations.

However, Jones says it is not himself that artists respect, but rather the power of music. "I've watched music break down barriers," he said. "'We Are the World' proved that. There is a power to positive examples. There is a power to effect change."[9]

It is that power, says Jones, that changed his life more than sixty years ago when he was a child in a poor section of Chicago's South Side. "I had big dreams when I was a little boy," he said. "If you're afraid to go chasing after your dreams, they're going to shrivel up, and so will you. You've got to create in your mind an invisible net underneath you, and jump."[10] That is exactly what Quincy Jones does.

2

LOFTY DREAMS,
THIRSTY MIND

Ⅰ n the 1991 documentary film *Listen Up: The Lives of Quincy Jones*, Jones walks into a broken-down brownstone apartment building at Thirty-sixth and Perry streets in Chicago. In one room, a bare lightbulb hangs from the ceiling. Paint is peeling off the walls. Everything looks exactly the same as it did fifty-some years ago, Jones says, as the camera zooms in on a window facing a brick wall. Trembling, he looks slowly around the room, reliving memories that only he knows. This room was his bedroom until he was eight years old.

Now Quincy Jones lives in a mansion in sunny Bel Air, California, surrounded by landscaped lawns, whispering palm trees, and kidney-shaped swimming pools. This is Jones's sanctuary, a place to escape from the world. His home has even been a safe haven for superstar singer Michael Jackson. Once, Jackson ran to Jones's house to escape a carload of fans chasing him in the streets.

Jones's two-story home sits high on a hill looking down on the estate of former president Ronald Reagan. This is very different from the bleak view of a red-brick wall and the dismal life in the ghetto of his childhood. Many years ago, young Quincy's view of life soared far beyond the ghetto—he had big dreams.

He was born Quincy Delight Jones, Jr., on March 14, 1933, in Chicago. Quincy's father, Quincy Delight Jones, Sr., had moved to Chicago from South Carolina to work as a carpenter and a semipro baseball player. Quincy's mother, Sarah, was from Mississippi. She was the daughter of a former slave.

This time period in America was a harsh one. A few years earlier, in 1929, the stock market had plummeted, causing what is known as the Great Depression. Much of the population was unemployed. Across the ocean in Germany, a dictator named Adolf Hitler was rounding up Jews and forcing them to work in slave labor camps. The world was just five years away from World War II and the Holocaust.

At the 1995 Academy Awards ceremony, Quincy Jones received the Jean Hersholdt Humanitarian Award. He had come a long way from his childhood in a Chicago ghetto. "You've got to dream real big," Jones once said.

Quincy Jones, Jr., recalled his childhood in inner-city Chicago: "We used to watch teachers getting killed and policemen shooting black teenagers in the back. Every street was a territory and every territory was run by a gang, and everybody used to carry a switchblade."[1]

Quincy Jones's mother, whom he remembers as flying into angry rages, suffered from a mental illness. When he was five, his mother smashed his birthday cake and ruined his birthday party. When Quincy was eight, tragedy struck. His mother had to be placed in a state mental institution. Ten years would pass before Quincy saw her again. Sadly, years later he discovered that his mother's illness may have been treatable. "It turned out what she really needed was only a lot of vitamin B," he told movie critic Roger Ebert of the *Chicago Sun-Times*.[2] Today he has forgiven her, but the pain of those memories lives fresh in his mind. "I never really knew what it was like to have a mother," says Jones. "There's no question that pushed me into a fantasy world. I used to sit for hours in my closet and just dream."[3]

Inside the walls of the Jones's tiny Chicago apartment, Quincy's dreams took him away from the realities of life. It was here that he first heard the delicate tinkling of piano keys played by a next-door neighbor named Lucy. The sounds drifted in through the open windows and the thin plaster walls. This was the first time he was aware that a human being could make music. In those days there were no boom boxes or CD players or even television. It was the simple melodies from a piano that began his love of music, a love that would someday take him out of poverty.

Although it seems that he now lives the lifestyle of the rich and famous, Jones knew poverty well. To this day he tells the story of one of the best meals he ever ate—a fried rat that his grandmother cooked for him.

His grandmother lived in Louisville, Kentucky, in a wooden shack that had a bent nail for a lock and kerosene lamps for light. When Quincy was a child, he and his younger brother, Lloyd, spent three summers with her. She often sent Quincy and Lloyd down to the Ohio River to catch a rat.

"We'd take that sucker home in a bag and she'd cook it up for supper," he once told a friend, the author Alex Haley. "She fried it with onions and it tasted good, man!"[4] That kind of memory, Jones says, makes one appreciate everything in life more. One of the joys in his life today is cooking gourmet meals for his friends, but he does not eat rats anymore.

Living for ten years in Chicago was hard, Quincy says. His father divorced his mother after she was admitted to the mental hospital. In 1943, Quincy Jones, Sr., married again. His new wife, Elvira, had three children from a previous marriage. (Eventually, the couple would have four children of their own, raising the number of children in their combined families to nine.) Within months of his father's remarriage, the Jones family moved to Bremerton, Washington—about forty-five minutes by ferry from Seattle and an entire world away from the ghetto.

Bremerton, a Navy town, was simmering with activity related to the war. Quincy Jones, Sr., was offered a good wartime job as a carpenter in the naval shipyards. Here was work and friendship. The Jones family settled in Sinclair Heights, a segregated housing project for African Americans. The town was built three miles downhill from the city, and no one in the project had telephones in their homes. Quincy learned years later it was planned this way because "they didn't want the black people to get so comfortable there after the war."[5]

In Chicago, Quincy accepted racism as a part of life. In Bremerton, the world was very different. "I entered school—the only black kid in the class—and the other kids were wonderful," he recalled. "Positively no problems." That was a stark contrast to Chicago, where segregation (and gang fighting) were common, Jones said. But the experience taught him that whether black or white, "kids are all alike," he says.[6]

Quincy's school had a music department with just about every kind of instrument available for the students to play. He experimented with many of them, playing one for a few months and then trying to learn another instrument. First, he played the French horn. He worked his way through piano, drums, and cymbals at Koontz Junior High, then played violin, tuba, baritone horn, E-flat alto horn, and trombone. At the age of twelve he discovered the trumpet, his final instrument.

He had no private lessons, although a local barber gave him some trumpet tips. He also had some instruction from the school music teacher, Joseph Powe, who had a dance band. It was Powe's dance band that ignited Quincy's passion for writing music. Although Quincy became an adequate trumpet player, it was his arranging, composing, and conducting skills that would propel him toward success years later. The time that young Quincy spent playing in Powe's band helped his talents grow.

"They had real music, written by hand, with numbers on it, and copied out, not like the stock music that's printed," said Quincy. "That was like big-time stuff, because that's what Woody Herman had. That's what Count Basie had."[7]

Often, Quincy would baby-sit for Powe's children. During those times he would read Powe's arranging books by Glenn Miller, mesmerized by how the trombones, saxes, and trumpets could fit together to make a chord. He was thirteen and in love with music. In fact, Quincy was fascinated with all kinds of music, whether it was a jazz band or the orchestral strings that accompanied the movies. He wanted to learn how to write movie music, too.

In 1947, the Jones family moved to Seattle. Fourteen-year-old Quincy played trumpet in the Garfield High School concert band. One of his best friends was a boy named Charlie Taylor, who put together a dance band. Quincy played in the band. Their first gig was at a YMCA and they were paid $7 apiece. Soon the band was working all over town. Quincy was playing trumpet, singing, even doing dance routines with the other band members. Then the little Taylor band became the opening act for well-known bands that would tour through Seattle. One day they were asked to play with one of the biggest jazz stars of the time—Billie Holiday.

Billie Holiday (1915–1959) was one of the greatest jazz singers who ever lived. The way she sang a melody was similar to the way a musician would play a melody. Through her voice, she could communicate the words to tunes as no other singer could. In the 1930s, she recorded with the very best jazz musicians, and she performed with several big bands throughout the country. Her downfall was her addiction to drugs, for which she served a prison sentence. Her singing career went progressively downhill, with a few recording exceptions, until she died in 1959 in a hospital in New York City.

Quincy Jones played with Billie Holiday in 1947,

one year before she would go to prison on drug charges. Even then, Quincy knew she was high on drugs. It made an impression on the teenager. He never forgot how badly the drugs affected her at the gig. "She could barely talk," says Jones. "I remember she didn't show up for rehearsals."[8]

Through working in the Taylor band, Quincy met trumpeter Clark Terry (born 1920), who was playing with Count Basie's band at the time. "Clark Terry, God bless him, taught me how to put my horn on my mouth right," said Jones.[9] In fact, whenever Terry performed in Seattle, young Quincy would ask Terry for a lesson. Sometimes Terry invited him backstage to see the big bands he played with. Terry also introduced Quincy to pianist/bandleader Count Basie. Terry, who now lives in New York City, still inspires musicians with his trumpet playing.

Meeting Count Basie was an important connection for young Quincy. William "Count" Basie (1904–1984) was a big-band leader for forty-five years. His style of piano playing was very simple, using just a few notes. But the notes he chose would swing with rhythm. Bill Basie was dubbed "the Count" by a radio announcer in Kansas City, Missouri, in the early 1930s.

Basie's band was called "the clock that swings" because it used an ensemble of musicians who could play with extreme dynamics—that is, both loud and soft playing—without compromising the time. With extreme dynamics, sometimes the band plays softer and softer and then suddenly roars with a loud blues line. The band plays together as if each player knows exactly what every other player is thinking. The Count Basie Orchestra still exists today and tours all over the world. It has the same high quality of musicians as when Count Basie was alive.

In 1947, Count Basie took Quincy under his wing. Basie became Quincy's friend and mentor. This relationship continued until Basie's death in 1984. It was Basie who performed one of Quincy's first arrangements, "Nocturne in Blue."

Having Basie use your arrangement was a big deal for anyone, but especially so for a fifteen-year-old boy. A big band was identified by its arrangements. The arrangements, known as charts, would reflect the personalities of the players and generally showcase the players' talents. For Basie to play Quincy's chart meant that he believed strongly in Quincy's talent.

The arranger is like a painter, using all the different sounds like a palette of colors. Quincy was learning a skill from the top giants in jazz who would someday help him be a producer of pop hits. Like the arrangers from the big-band era, good pop music producers highlight a singer's talents—knowing what kind of range or tune the singer sounds best with, and which tunes or styles are best left alone. Quincy was developing all these skills before his seventeenth birthday.

There was one teen in Seattle who affected Quincy perhaps more than any of the stars—seventeen-year-old Ray Charles. Although Ray Charles was not much older than Quincy, it seemed to Quincy that Charles was light-years ahead of him. Charles played in dance clubs with his own trio, arranged music for bands, and lived in his own apartment. Ray Charles was also blind.

Ray Charles Robinson, now known as Ray Charles (born 1932), taught himself to play piano by age three and lost his sight at the age of seven. Orphaned at age sixteen, he left school to work professionally as a musician. By age twenty-four, he had recorded forty singles and signed a contract with Atlantic Records. By 1962, his record sales had reached $8 million, an extraordinary amount at the time.

Today he is a living legend and has influenced everyone from the Beatles to Billy Joel. Joel named his daughter Alexa Ray in honor of Charles. Ray Charles has won Kennedy Center honors and the Grammy's Lifetime Achievement Award. He is also in the Rock and Roll Hall of Fame.

Quincy attached himself to Charles. The two became as close as brothers. Charles taught Quincy about voicings and chords and how to write arrangements for horns. He showed Quincy that each horn has a distinctive sound. From that point on,

Quincy was hooked on the idea of orchestration and arranging.

Arranging and composing was always more important to Quincy than playing his trumpet. In fact, in one of the first articles ever written about Quincy, he told a reporter from *The Spectator*, the Seattle University newspaper, that he wanted to learn how to write "mood music," that is, music for movies.[10] Quincy Jones was eighteen years old at the time. A decade later that same desire would take him to Hollywood.

With every big band that came through town, Quincy would be there, hanging out with the band members, trying to sit in. Sometimes he would sneak backstage at a concert by putting his trumpet under his arm and walking quickly past the security guards. This was how he first met Clark Terry. It was also how he met vibraphonist/bandleader Lionel Hampton.

Lionel Hampton (born 1913) became famous for playing the vibes. His music had a swing feel and a strong adherence to beat. While he was in college he began playing with the Benny Goodman Quartet and his solos soon became legendary. Hampton formed his own big band in the early 1930s, with the very best jazz musicians he could find on trumpet, saxophone, and trombone. The energy that Hampton poured out on the bandstand would excite not only the musicians but the audience as well. It also caught the imagination of young Quincy Jones.

"Lionel Hampton was a superstar back then," Quincy said. "He had the first rock-n-roll band in America . . . with that big-beat sound and that honking tenor sax and the screaming high-note trumpet. Hamp was a *showman*."[11]

Quincy's idols were the jazz giants like Lionel Hampton and Count Basie. Quincy and his other musician friends did not desire to be rich, Jones said. The goal was just to be "good and recognized as a good musician, that's what we lived for."[12]

While Quincy was still in high school, Hampton hired him to go on the road with the band as a trumpet player and music arranger. Quincy packed his bag and raced to the band bus, holding his trumpet tightly. This would be his first gig on a big-time jazz band. But it was not to be. Before the bus pulled away, Hampton's wife, Gladys, yanked Quincy off the bus and told him he would not be hired until he had graduated from high school.

That turn of events was a blessing in disguise, Jones said later. "I was *highly* motivated to finish school so I could join that band."[13] He stayed in school, dated his high school sweetheart, Jeri Caldwell, and kept studying music. In less than a year, his dream of playing in Lionel Hampton's band would come true.

3

PLAY TRUMPET, SEE THE WORLD

ighteen-year-old Quincy Jones's musical suite "The Four Winds" won him a scholarship to Seattle University. But after one semester he was disappointed with the school's music program. It seemed "a little bit square," he said.[1] He longed to be in New York City, where it seemed all his musical idols were playing.

One day he opened up an envelope from Schillinger House (now Berklee College of Music) in Boston, Massachusetts. It was a letter offering a scholarship to a world of music three thousand miles away! This was the key to his future. He had a lot to learn about music, and Boston was very close to the center of it all—New York City. This time when he packed his bags to leave, no one stopped him. Quincy Jones left Seattle with his trumpet and his high school sweetheart, Jeri Caldwell.

Berklee College of Music was as close to heaven as young Jones could imagine. Nowhere else on earth could he immerse himself in ten hours of classes a day, write a piece of music, and find musicians who would play his arrangements anytime day or night. Jones was not the only musician who felt this way. At Berklee, there were hundreds of other people who loved music just as much as he did. There was camaraderie and competition all in one place.

Jones was a sponge, soaking up as much music knowledge as possible. There was so much to learn as a player and as an arranger. The popular music of the day was swing, but a new form of music was also emerging—bebop. Bebop is much more challenging than swing. Rhythms are faster. Instead of playing melodies, the musician uses the chords of the tune to show his or her talent.

Many musicians who loved swing hated bebop. Even audiences that respected the musicians often found bebop difficult to follow. For the beboppers, it did not matter if the audience could not follow along. Bebop belonged to the musicians. The music was challenging and it stretched their playing skills. Jones struggled to master the style.

Bebop was not just a style of music. Like hip-hop today, bebop was an attitude toward life. Beboppers were hip. They had their own fashions. A good example was trumpeter Dizzy Gillespie, who always wore a beret and had a goatee.

Gillespie (1917–1993) was one of the greats in the world of jazz. He was nicknamed "Dizzy" because of his comical antics on stage. Gillespie was also famous for his strange trumpet. In 1953, someone had fallen on Gillespie's trumpet and bent the bell upward. Gillespie liked the sound and began having trumpets built for him that way.

Gillespie played in big bands all his life and is often referred to as the "Ambassador of Jazz" because he was known and loved by so many people. Gillespie and another musician, Charlie "Bird" Parker, were the innovators of bebop. Saxophonist Parker (1920–1955), often called "the father of bebop," was one of the greatest jazz musicians who ever lived.

Tragically, some of the beboppers used drugs, often with terrible results. Gillespie did not use drugs, but Parker did. When Parker died, a medical examiner from the New York City coroner's office had to guess at Parker's age for the death certificate. By Parker's appearance, the doctor placed him between fifty and sixty years of age. Parker was just thirty-four.[2] Parker was nicknamed "Bird" because once, on the way to a gig, his car had hit a chicken in the road. He picked up the chicken, carried it with him to his gig, and asked his hosts to cook it for him. His name has inspired many jazz clubs: for example, Birdland in New York City and Birdhouse in Chicago.

Parker was the first musician to play bebop. He played lightning-fast solos with complex harmonic changes and chromatic runs. He changed accents on downbeats to upbeats, and then changed them back to simple melodies—all in the course of one solo. His style of playing is still popular today in the jazz world. Countless professionals and music students imitate Parker's sound. When Parker died, the words "Bird Lives" appeared in subway stations throughout New York City. With Parker and others, Quincy Jones saw once more how drugs ruined some of the greatest musicians. This was an important education for him.

Jones enjoyed the performances of the Lionel Hampton Big Band. Hampton was steeped in the swing style and he was a master performer. He knew how to get the crowd excited and involved in his shows. A typical show would open with a tap dancer, a vocal quartet, then a comic before the big band even took the stage. Hampton also had his band wear outlandish purple outfits, with matching coats, underwear, and socks. The band even wore big purple hats. Jones knew it was corny. As a member of Hampton's band, though, he would learn a lot.

Finally, Hampton invited Jones to join his band. So, after one year at Berklee, Jones left school in 1951 for the best education a music student could get—the real world of performing. The first stop was New York City.

Jones loved New York City, with all its sights and sounds, subway trains rumbling beneath the streets, sirens wailing, and hordes of people on the move. Jones was where his idols lived and worked and played. He met many of jazz's greatest musicians, including Dizzy Gillespie and Charlie "Bird" Parker.

Hampton's band did not stay in New York City for long periods. The band did most of its performing on the road. Working in any big band on the road is always a grueling experience. Like many other big bands, the Lionel Hampton Big Band played concerts, then packed up and traveled to the next town to do it all over again. Often, the band slept in the bus, saving money on hotel expenses. It is very expensive to travel with an eighteen-piece big band. Even today, traveling bands still often play one concert and travel to the next concert without stopping to spend the night and rest. In musician slang, these dates are called "hit-and-runs."

After leaving New York in 1951, the Hampton band went on a long tour through the South, playing seventy-nine "hit-and-runs" just in the Carolinas

On the road in 1951 with Lionel Hampton's band. From left to right: Art Farmer, eighteen-year-old Quincy Jones, Lionel Hampton, and Walter Williams.

alone. For Jones, this road experience in the early 1950s was more than just a musical education. Traveling through the segregated South, he saw firsthand how racism affected even such everyday tasks as eating a meal. Because Jones had been living in Seattle, he had never experienced segregation through the Jim Crow laws before. These were laws that allowed the separation of the races: Blacks and whites had separate schools, restaurants, streetcars, hospitals, cemeteries, and even restrooms and drinking fountains.

Jones was traveling with the Hampton band in 1951, years before Jim Crow laws came to an end. African Americans were not served meals in many places, so the band had a white bus driver just so the musicians could eat while they were on tour. The driver was able to get food for the band at road stops that would not serve African Americans. Although Jones got used to the hardships of traveling, he says he never got used to the discrimination against people of color. "You couldn't stay in white hotels and to me, coming from Seattle, a lot of this stuff was like a slap in the face," Jones said. "Even in Philadelphia they had segregated hotels."[3]

Racism seemed to be everywhere, Jones remembered. One night the band arrived in a Texas town where they were horrified to see an effigy of an African-American man hanging from a church steeple.

An effigy is a crude image of a person. Sometimes it looks like a scarecrow that might resemble a famous person. Usually the image is treated with hatred—burned, ripped, or hanged.

Seeing the effigy of a black man really shook Jones up. The older musicians in the band told him that discrimination happened to all African Americans, no matter how famous they were. Even in Las Vegas, top entertainers like Sammy Davis, Jr., Lena Horne, and Harry Belafonte were not allowed to stay at the hotels, eat in the restaurants, or mingle with the crowds at the very places where people paid hundreds of dollars to see them perform. They were kept separate just because of the color of their skin.

For Jones, knowing that famous people also suffered did not make the discrimination easier to accept. The older men told him there was one place where discrimination did not seem to exist for blacks—that place was Europe. Jones learned that the band was scheduled for a three-month tour abroad. This would be the beginning of a very different road experience for him.

In Europe, the band was treated to standing ovations and cheering crowds. By this time Jones was writing arrangements and original charts of music for the Hampton band. Often he wrote long into the night after the band had performed a concert. Here, the "hit-and-runs" were few. He had more time to write music.

In addition to writing for the eighteen-piece Hampton band, Jones was also arranging pieces for bands of different sizes: sextets (piano, bass, drums, saxophone, trumpet, and trombone), septets (piano, bass, drums, and four wind instruments), and octets (piano, bass, drums, and five wind instruments). He also wrote arrangements for another big band that consisted of European and American musicians. Jones recorded this music in secret because Lionel Hampton had a rule that no one in his band was allowed to record in Europe with anyone except him. If any musicians were caught doing this, they would immediately be fired, with no return ticket to the United States.

Jones and several other members of the Hampton band broke this rule—often. Sometimes they had to sneak out of their hotel after midnight. When they left their hotel rooms for a recording session, they would leave one by one at different times so no one else in the band would notice. Once, Jones and bandmates Clifford Brown and Art Farmer went to a recording session by climbing down a fire escape. The Hampton road manager was sitting in the hotel lobby like a sentry on guard duty.

Jones and some other members of the Hampton band secretly recorded several albums while they were in Europe. A recording of Jones's tune "Stockholm Sweetnin' " became a jazz classic, with performances by trumpeters Brown and Farmer along with the European band known as the Swedish-American All Stars.

The Hampton European tour ended and the band flew back to the United States. Jones and eleven band members promptly quit when they arrived. They knew they would have been fired anyway as soon as their secretly recorded albums were released to the public.

Jones was also tired of the road. He wanted to live in New York City and pursue his dream of working as a musician. Jones wanted to settle into domestic life with Jeri Caldwell. But making the transition from being a traveling road musician to the daily grind of earning a living would not be easy.

4

THE AMBASSADOR
OF JAZZ

ones had traveled with the Lionel
Hampton Big Band for almost three years
before he left and settled in New York. It
was difficult for him to leave, because the band had
felt like a family to him. However, it was not long
before he was the head of his own family: In 1953, Jeri
Caldwell had a baby girl they named Jolie. Now Jones
needed work to support them. New York City was an
expensive place to live.

Jones began arranging music for many musicians.
He arranged tunes for James Moody, a saxophonist,

and sometimes did arrangements for his trumpet mentor, Clark Terry. Other times Jones played trumpet himself at commercial recording sessions. Sometimes he wrote for R&B (rhythm and blues) bands and for singers such as Dinah Washington.

Jones also wrote music for Ray Anthony and Tommy Dorsey, both leaders of popular big bands. Dorsey and his band played on a television show in the summer of 1955. Jones arranged Dorsey's scores. This was Jones's first television gig. One day, a young singer named Elvis Presley took the stage. Jones told a writer that "the guys in the band just wanted to die when he came up for the first time, because he couldn't sing in tempo. The band couldn't play with him . . . and they had to send him to Nashville to get some dudes to play with him because he couldn't understand time."[1] Jones nicknamed Elvis Presley "Elvis Depresley."

Elvis Presley went on to become the "King of Rock and Roll." Even though he died in 1976, his fans still flock to his hometown of Memphis, Tennessee, to see Graceland, their musical idol's home.

In 1956, trumpeter Dizzy Gillespie asked Jones to help him put together an all-star big band. The State Department wanted to send a jazz band to the Middle East to promote goodwill toward Americans. The United States government was supplying enough money to pay for generous salaries to each "sideman" (musician in the band) and for all the band's travel and food costs. Even today, a gig paying all these expenses would be amazing. It was also important that the United States government was recognizing jazz as a cultural export just like any other national treasure. Jazz is an original American art form.

Gillespie asked Jones to write the arrangements for the group as well. And since Gillespie was too busy to help before the tour began, all the organizing of the band fell on Jones's shoulders. He had to select the musicians, rehearse the band, choose the music, and write the arrangements. Gillespie planned to join them in Rome once the tour actually began.

This was a difficult time for Jones. Besides juggling all the details of the tour, he also ran into other problems. Several of the sidemen he had hired canceled just before the tour began. The key to having a great big band is to have great musicians fill every spot. Now some important spots were empty.

Many musicians called Jones, asking to join his band, but Jones wanted only the very best. In addition, he had one more problem with selecting members. He had to make sure that all the musicians selected could also get along together. "A collection of great performers don't of necessity make a great team—if they can't get on together as human beings," he said.[2]

The band turned out to be a group of highly disciplined musicians who even showed up in blizzards to rehearse. All of them got their passports and their immunizations in order before the tour began. Because of their enthusiasm, the group came together as a band.

So it was that in 1956 the Middle East "World Statesmen Tour" began. Jones and Dizzy Gillespie led a sixteen-piece band of goodwill ambassadors of jazz into the hotspots of the world: Iran, Pakistan, Lebanon, Syria, Turkey, Yugoslavia, and Greece.

The musicians were almost as astonished to see the Middle Eastern cities as the people living there were to hear and see jazz played. One of the strongest impressions for the musicians was the poverty they observed. For example, saxophonist Ernie Wilkins lost his saxophone and needed one in the city of Abadan, Iran. He discovered that saxophonists there used the same reed in their instruments for a whole year. In the United States, most saxophonists use a new reed every few days.

During the tour Dizzy Gillespie rode a camel. Another time he donned a white turban and charmed a snake while playing a snake charmer's pipe. He had a sense of humor and he was a very caring person. In Ankara, Turkey, he refused to play a concert at a diplomat's garden party until the poor children who were crowding around outside the walls were allowed inside to listen.

There is a saying that music is an international language. Nowhere was this proved more true than

In 1956, during the "World Statesmen Tour," Jones sits at the Parthenon in Athens, Greece.

during this tour. In Greece, when the band arrived, people were throwing stones at the United States Embassy. Dizzy Gillespie wrote about this in his book *To BE, or not . . . to BOP.* He said that in spite of the near-riot at the embassy, he decided to go on with the concert because the musicians weren't involved with the politics. "We came to serve the people, not to use them," Gillespie wrote. So the show went on.[3]

After the performance, he was grabbed by the audience and (in a fifties version of crowd surfing) tossed into the air and passed along people's shoulders. Gillespie feared for his life. People were screaming at him in Greek, but then he heard some familiar words: *Bravo, bravo.* "I knew we were a big hit then in Athens," he said.[4]

In Pakistan, the people had never seen a trombone. Many countries in the Middle East practice the religion of Islam. The people who practice this faith, Muslims, believe that a woman should dress so that only her hands, face, and feet are seen. One of the band members was a woman, trombonist Melba Liston, and the audience was very surprised to see her playing the trombone, let alone not wearing a veil, Jones said.

Liston (born 1926) was for many years the only woman in the United States who played jazz trombone professionally on a par with male musicians.[5] She played in the bands of Count Basie, Dizzy Gillespie, and Quincy Jones, co-led a group with Clark Terry, and orchestrated music for Gillespie, Duke Ellington, Count Basie, Al Grey, and Dinah Washington. During the "World Statesmen Tour" she was responsible for writing a musical summation of the styles and sounds of jazz. It was a history of the music. Liston, who now lives in California, continues to play her trombone. Her arranging talents are still in demand to this day.

The musicians learned a great deal from their experiences in the Middle East. Jones learned that music was universal, that it bypassed language, politics, and cultural differences. A few months later the band again went on tour, this time to South America. After that tour, Jones left the band to stay home with his family.

Not long after he left the band, Jones, then twenty-four, was chosen as New Star Arranger of 1956 by a readers' poll in a Paris, France, music magazine. It was the first of many awards he would receive in his long career. Next, a record producer at ABC-Paramount asked Jones to make a record of his own jazz works under his own name. The album, *This Is How I Feel About Jazz*, was produced in September 1956.

In spite of his album, Jones was frustrated with the racism that he faced in the recording studios in New York City. African-American arrangers were allowed to oversee the rhythm sections and horns, but they were

Quincy Jones in 1956, the year his album *This Is How I Feel About Jazz* was produced.

not considered skilled enough to write for strings. This decision was based solely on skin color. Jones knew he could write just as well for strings as he could for other instruments. Often, another arranger would be brought in just to write the orchestral segments, cheating Jones out of better pay. This was about to change.

A French record company, Barclay Disque, in Paris, asked Jones to become its musical director. The company was founded and run by Eddie and Nicole Barclay, who were big fans of Jones's from his Lionel Hampton days in Europe. It was an impressive gig for Jones because they were entrusting him with running the entire company—including writing string parts. In 1957, Jones moved his family to Paris, agreeing to stay several months. He ended up staying three years.

This opportunity also allowed him to study composition with Nadia Boulanger. Boulanger was a famous classical music teacher who had taught the legendary composers Aaron Copland and Igor Stravinsky. Boulanger was a mentor to Jones. She introduced him to such famous people as author Richard Wright, artist Pablo Picasso, and singer/dancer Josephine Baker.

This was an important time in Jones's life. Although he had experience working in big bands and arranging for jazz groups, he had little classical music instruction. Now he was studying under strict standards from teacher Boulanger. Years later, Boulanger would say that her two most distinguished pupils were classical composer Igor Stravinsky and Quincy Jones.[6]

At the French record company, Jones was permitted to use string instruments in his compositions if he desired. The recording studios in New York had been reluctant to do this. Jones now saw firsthand how a successful record company was run. This was the year that he wrote the music for Count Basie's next album, *Basie One More Time*. He wrote and arranged other important albums as well. *Birth of a Band*, featuring his old mentor Clark Terry and Hampton band member Art Farmer, was also recorded. Jones also arranged the album *Count Basie With Strings*, a session with Count Basie and singer Billy Eckstine.

Eckstine (1914–1995) was one of the first African-American pop idols. His rich, bass-baritone voice and perfect pitch made him a leader in the field of the romantic ballad. His voice influenced many of the bebop singers. After leading his own big band, called "the incubator of bebop," Eckstine crossed over from jazz to pop stardom in the late 1940s. Jones was fifteen years old when he first met Eckstine. He said later that Eckstine was "the most beautiful-looking man you ever saw in your life. . . . He didn't sing dumb 'oogum boogum' songs, he sang pretty melodies that had meaningful words. There was an incredible element of

Quincy Jones directs the music at the recording session of the album *Birth of a Band*.

class and taste involved at all times. . . . And he was very hip and stylish."[7]

The year 1957 was a good year for Jones. He was learning and building his confidence as a writer, arranger, and producer. In 1958 he was asked to be the musical director of a new blues opera called *Free and Easy.* The composer was Harold Arlen, the same musician who had written the music for *The Wizard of Oz* in 1939. Jones was to assemble a "dream-team" big band, arrange the music, break in the show throughout Europe, pick up singer/dancer Sammy Davis, Jr., in London, and take the show to Broadway in New York City.

Unfortunately, within weeks after the "dream-team" of musicians was flown to Paris, the show folded. The musicians could not leave because France was fighting a war of independence with its colony Algeria. No one could get out of France.

Jones was responsible for paying the band members. Top musicians from New York City, along with their families, had moved to France just to work for the show. Now they were stranded. For ten months, Jones struggled every week to make the $5,000 payroll just to keep the musicians afloat. The band would play one-nighters in Sweden, a week's worth of gigs in France, and then go back to Sweden. Jones sold the publishing rights to many of his compositions to cover the bill, but the pressure was getting to him. It was a difficult time.

It took courage to carry on. Eventually Jones managed to scrape together the money and send the band home, but he was in debt from this for years. His bad luck would soon change with a phone call.

5

A Once-in-a-Lifetime Break

he voice on the other end of the phone one day in 1961 was Irving Green, the president of Mercury Records. He and Jones were good friends. Green had been watching Jones for several years, both as a friend and as a businessman. It was not just Green's business skills that earned him the presidency of the company—it was also his eye for talent.

To Green, it did not matter that the show *Free and Easy* had failed. Broadway shows come and go in the music business. What Green noticed was the music

Jones composed and arranged for several big bands and singers. Jones was nominated for a Grammy Award in 1959 for Best Jazz Performance for the album *The Great Wide World of Quincy Jones* and in 1961 for his band arrangement of "Let the Good Times Roll" for his friend Ray Charles. Singer Dinah Washington loved Jones's writing and praised him whenever she was asked to name her favorite arranger. Green took notice of all this.

He called Jones to offer him a job at Mercury Records as both a staff arranger and an A&R (artist and repertoire) person who picks new artists and chooses what they sing. Green also offered to teach Jones the business side of record producing.

For Jones, this was like going back to school. Wearing a suit and tie, he went to work every morning at 9:00 A.M. Green taught Jones about business details like administration, office routines, artist relations, dealing with difficult agents, and cutting and mastering records. He encouraged Jones to put his talent as a musician to work as a record producer.

"I started to pay back my bread [from the *Free and Easy* flop], and I learned the music business backwards and forwards," said Jones. "Mercury . . . gave us executive courses, which showed me what it was all about: as artists, we're just another serial number in a profit and loss log."[1]

Jones learned not to fear the business part of music. In fact, he learned it so well that years later he would use it to expand his music career. He now manages his own companies in records, video, and multimedia. Few musicians make this leap into the corporate world. As Jones explains: "Artists think on one level, while corporate thinking is on a really different level." Jones's five years at Mercury were an "educational trip."[2]

Jones got a new nickname: "Q." Soon he started producing records for jazz artists such as singer Sarah Vaughan, trumpeter Dizzy Gillespie, and drummer Art Blakey. He also put together another big band. Musicians are always forming new bands. This band played occasionally at jazz festivals and concerts in New York City. Mercury Records produced some of the band's albums. Jones was becoming more in demand by singers who wanted him to both arrange and produce their albums.

Although the records he was producing got great critical reviews, they were not hits in the popular music world. Mercury challenged him to find new pop talent. Taking them up on the challenge, he sorted through a stack of demos—samples sent in by new artists—on his desk and heard the bright, happy voice of a young teenager from New Jersey. Leslie Gore was not a jazz singer, but she did sing on key and she was attractive, which is important in the world of show business.

Jones found a couple of tunes he thought Gore could sing. One Saturday morning they recorded the songs. A few days later he ran into another record producer, who had mentioned that he was releasing a tune, "It's My Party," with one of *his* groups. It was one of the songs that Jones had recorded with Gore! Realizing he had to get his version out first, Jones raced back to his office. He made a hundred copies of Gore singing "It's My Party" and mailed them to radio stations across the country that day.

A few weeks later, the tune hit number one on the charts. Jones had scored his first hit record in the pop industry and gave Mercury Records one of its biggest successes in the company's history. In her recording career, Gore had two songs sell a million copies: "It's My Party" and "You Don't Own Me."[3] Several months after Gore's first hit single, Jones won his first Grammy for his arrangement of the tune "I Can't Stop Loving You" for the Count Basie Orchestra. Ray Charles had made the song a hit a year earlier.

Jones was now deluged with writing offers from top singers, both male and female. He was also promoted to the position of vice president at Mercury Records— the first black in the United States to hold such a job in a white-owned industry.

Working in this position gave him an insider's view of the racism in the music industry. "Oh, man," Jones says. "There is so much blood on that path. Kids today

Quincy Jones discovered singer Leslie Gore and produced her single "It's My Party." The song hit number one and was Jones's first big hit in the pop industry.

don't realize how things were. . . . I was right there when a record would be made by the Penguins (an African-American group) and they'd rush it over to the Crew Cuts and use the same arrangement for the white market. Fats Domino to Pat Boone, Big Mama Thornton to Elvis—it goes back to Benny Goodman and Basie. . . . It's been going on forever."[4]

Jones worked hard in his position as a record executive. In 1963 alone, he logged twenty-five thousand miles traveling to Holland, Italy, Great Britain, and Japan to represent Mercury's interests. He worked a total of five years for Mercury (1961–1965). In those five years he quit playing his trumpet, but he was building a reputation for being a success not only in the jazz world but in the pop world as well.

With his impressive list of arranging credits, Jones now wanted to try arranging in another art form that he had loved since childhood—movie music. In 1961, he began writing his first movie score for a Swedish movie, *The Boy in the Tree*.

In fact, Mercury gave Jones a two-month leave to write the score for a second movie (and his first American movie), *The Pawnbroker*. The movie was about a former Nazi who was haunted by his memories. Although the film did not do well at the box office, it was another important career step for Jones.

It was also a first for an African American. Few African Americans had written any music for the movies. Encouraged by his experience with *The Pawnbroker*, Jones was thinking about moving to Hollywood and finding a job with one of the major movie studios. That was when his phone rang once again.

This time it was an offer to arrange music for a big band and a singer, to conduct the music for a record, and then to go on the road to promote it on a nationwide tour. The singer was Frank Sinatra and the big band was the Count Basie Orchestra. No musician would turn down such an opportunity. No one at Mercury objected to Jones's taking this work. It was a once-in-a-lifetime opportunity.

Suddenly Jones was putting in very long hours arranging jazz music once again. This time he was working for one of the best big bands, the Count Basie Orchestra, and one of the greatest singers in the world, Frank Sinatra.

Frank Sinatra (born 1915), nicknamed "Old Blue Eyes," is a legend in the music business. Instrumentalists from bass trombone players to drummers study how this master sings. Sinatra sings the tempo just right, placing the melody in the "pocket." ("Pocket" is a musician's term for where the rhythm feels right.) He phrases words and melodies perfectly with the chord changes. He has made famous

In 1965, Quincy Jones was selected as the musician to arrange the music and conduct the tour of singer Frank Sinatra with the Count Basie Orchestra. For Jones, it was one of the most exciting times of his life.

such songs as "New York, New York," "I Did It My Way," and "Fly Me to the Moon." In 1965 the legendary Sinatra was in top form.

The combination of Sinatra and Basie was electric. It produced some of the greatest music ever recorded: songs such as "The Best Is Yet to Come" and "Too Marvelous for Words." As conductor, Jones said, "I've never been so excited about going to work every night."[5]

At the end of the tour, Jones decided to move to Hollywood. The decision was an ambitious one. No African American had ever written more than just an occasional score for a major movie company, but Jones had reached high for his goals before when chasing his dreams.

"I left New York and just jumped in," he said. "I guess part of it is the adventure and the excitement, the danger of jumping into areas you don't really know. . . . it's not really for real, but it is for real. And you can get back out."[6]

However, his professional success was expensive to his personal life. The long hours of work and the weeks and weeks of being away from his family were hard. When he resigned from Mercury Records in 1965, he also divorced his wife, Jeri. Their daughter, Jolie, stayed in New York with her mother. Jones had put his career first.

Writing movie music was an exciting dream that

Jones wanted to experience. He thought he had a chance to make inroads into the profession. After all, he had won one Grammy and his music was nominated for several more. He had also created a major pop star and conducted legends in the music business. Jones thought he had paid his dues in the music industry and proved he was talented. But work came slowly at first in Hollywood. For one whole year he had no job offers.

6

HOLLYWOOD
APARTHEID

Ever since he was a child, Jones had loved the movies. It was the music that breathed life into the film's images. Jones's ears were awakened every time he saw—or, rather, heard—a movie. When he was fifteen, he read and reread a book by Frank Skinner titled *Underscore*, a book about film music writing. Back then, all the movie studios used a master musician who set the studio's style. Jones could close his eyes and tell by the music which movie studio made the film, perhaps Paramount, or MGM.

Writing movie scores was a dream Jones kept hidden for years because he was not sure he could do it. Now, with two movies under his belt, he knew he could. But there was a problem bigger than learning how to write the movie scores: Hollywood had never hired an African-American musician to write a major movie score.

In fact, in the early 1960s there were not very many African Americans in Hollywood, except for a few actors. The most prominent one, Eddie Anderson, played a stereotyped character named Rochester, who was a sidekick of the comedian Jack Benny. Anderson often played the part of a grinning chauffeur or butler. There were no African Americans working in most other areas of moviemaking—producing, scriptwriting, and music composing. The top positions were held exclusively by whites. Jones had broken down barriers before. He had to try again.

He carefully weighed the decision to enter into this new career. He knew some people in Hollywood. After all, he was the conductor of the Frank Sinatra/Count Basie concerts. He had also won a Grammy, produced several gold records, studied classical orchestration with the world-renowned teacher Nadia Boulanger, and written two movie scores (the Swedish film and the American movie *The Pawnbroker*). Jones had worked not only at a successful record company but also on a failed musical venture, the blues opera *Free and Easy*. These projects had taught him a lot about how the business worked. His move to Hollywood was not foolish, but it was gutsy.

Finally, Jones received his first big Hollywood offer, to write the music for a movie called *Mirage*. He almost lost the contract when it was discovered that he was African American. "The people at Universal freaked out when they got a look at me, because they didn't know that I was black," said Jones. "I don't think they'd seen many blacks around there, except maybe in the kitchen, and they tried to bail out of it."[1]

One of Jones's friends, the composer Henry Mancini, fought for Jones behind closed doors, saying that he knew Jones could do it. *Mirage*, starring Gregory Peck, was released in 1966. Although the movie was not a financial success, Jones had made his presence known.

More film and television scores followed for Jones. Often, his was the only black face among the sea of white faces as the executives sat in the darkened movie editing rooms.

Of the few African Americans in Hollywood, two others besides Jones stood out. One was Sydney Poitier, an African American who was popular with both white and black movie audiences. Poitier, who had won an Academy Award in 1963, did not sing or tell jokes. Instead, he had a cool demeanor that many Americans loved. Jones was hired to write the music for the movie *The Slender Thread*, starring Poitier.

Another African American who was opening Hollywood doors at the same time as Jones was actor/comedian Bill Cosby. Co-starring in *I Spy*, he became the first African-American actor to star in a dramatic television series.

Poitier, Cosby, and Jones were three key figures in breaking down stereotypes and prejudices in Hollywood. All three worked together. By the end of the 1960s, Jones had scored four Poitier movies: *In the Heat of the Night, For Love of Ivy, The Lost Man,* and *Brother John.* He also wrote the theme for Cosby's first television situation comedy, *The Bill Cosby Show,* in 1969.

One of the goals for any musician writing a television or movie theme is to make the main melody memorable so that anyone who hears it once will never forget it. Jones was the first arranger to use a synthesizer in a television score. For the television series *Ironside,* he used a synthesizer to produce a police siren in the main melody line and heavy brass sounds to suggest the violence to come.

With his jazz background, Jones brought a fresh approach to the movie music world. Before Quincy Jones, the scores tended to be grandiose and overwhelming. Jones has an ear for popular tastes of the day. He brought his big-band arranging techniques (that is, the small-group sound within a big group) and added his own touch to the scores: "I feel I brought the

Quincy Jones wrote music for several movies that starred actor Sydney Poitier. Jones, Poitier, and comedian/actor Bill Cosby were key figures in breaking down prejudices and stereotypes of African Americans in Hollywood.

sensibility of modern Rhythm and Blues influences to scoring. Incorporating it with the dramatic scoring . . . it's a kind of hybrid art."[2] Jones brought that hybrid skill to television. Anyone hearing the funky theme to the television series *Sanford and Son* can hear the strong R&B influence.

For Jones's first Hollywood movie project he incorporated street sounds into the movie—another unique approach. Jones could write in a classical European style as well. One movie score that he considers his best was *In Cold Blood*.

This movie was about the brutal murder of a family in Kansas. It is a chilling true story, written by Truman Capote. Jones wrote large orchestral backgrounds for some scenes, blues in others, and just percussion and bass in still others. Although the soundtrack was nominated for a Grammy Award in 1967, it did not win.

Jones mastered the art of writing music for movies and television. He has advice for would-be composers: "The movies are a fine workshop and a proving ground that you'll never come across working on records. Just the idea of dramatic scenes; they force you into musical situations that one might never get into otherwise."[3] For example, Jones said that a composer must be flexible enough to write music for a murder scene one moment, and then quickly shift into a peaceful scene in the next. Music for the movies can be very challenging.

In 1965, Jones, age thirty-two, married a Swedish model, Ulla Anderson, who was nineteen. In 1966 they had a baby girl named Martina-Lisa. In 1968, they had a baby boy, Quincy Delight Jones III. Throughout this time, Jones was writing as many as eight movie scores a year and the music for several television shows. "I was under a lot of pressure," he said. "I was staying up five and six nights writing scores. I was smoking tons, up to four packs a day."[4] Eventually, his lifestyle would catch up with him.

Although Jones loved writing some of the movie scores, the work was not always enjoyable. Writing memorable themes was fun, but writing music for scenes that needed help from the music to create emotions was not fun at all. Grinding out this kind of music was grueling. As busy as Jones was, he longed for creative freedom. He missed arranging and producing music albums.

In 1969, he was asked to record a big-band album for A&M. After all the movie scores he had written, recording again was like a breath of fresh air. It took him just two weeks to assemble the right group of musicians for his album *Walking in Space*. He clearly made the right choices: *Walking in Space* won a Grammy in 1970 for best jazz performance by a large group.

In 1969, Jones began recording for A&M Records with the album
Walking in Space, which won a Grammy that same year.

At the end of the 1960s, Jones was busy working as a record producer, jazz composer and arranger, and movie/television film scorer. He was on top of the music business. His music was literally out of this world. When astronauts Neil Armstrong and Edwin "Buzz" Aldrin, Jr., took their historic first steps on the moon in July 1969, Aldrin popped in a cassette tape. It was *Fly Me to the Moon*, which Jones had arranged and conducted for Count Basie and Frank Sinatra. Years later, Aldrin told Jones the story when they met at a party. Jones was stunned. "The first music played on the moon," he said. "I freaked!"[5]

7

BRAIN DRAIN

or decades, Jones worked very long and hard hours. He threw himself into musical projects, often staying up for days at a time. Jones liked to write through the night because he thought he could get more accomplished.

"But the real reason I write and arrange at such weird hours is the psychological effect it has on being creative," he said. "After you get past a certain point, your subconscious mind comes out. It breaks through all your artistic fears and inhibitions."[1]

By 1974, Jones's career was in high gear. He had

composed, arranged, or produced more than 106 music albums by different artists. He had written the film scores for thirty-two movies. He had won two Grammys and was nominated for dozens more.

His personal life was less successful. His marriage to Ulla Anderson ended in divorce. He then dated television actress Peggy Lipton, who would become his next wife. They were happy, although life was hectic. For Jones, there was always another score to write or another album to produce.

In June 1974, he released the pop album *Body Heat.* He had not been involved in the pop world since working with singer Leslie Gore. *Body Heat* was a first for Jones in that it was not a jazz album. "I tried to express the music that I feel," said Jones. "Critically, I received some grief from my die-hard jazz friends but on the whole it was well received."[2]

A reviewer from the *Detroit Free-Press* wrote that the album was "Quincy Jones' most commercial album to date [and] one of the most satisfying ones artistically." Other critics described it as "solid," "soul-filled," "sensuous," "intense," and "cool," with "an undercurrent of slowly burning fire." The album, which contained the songs "Soul Saga," "Everything Must Change," and "If I Ever Lose This Heaven," was a huge success. Sales topped a million and the album stayed on the top-five lists of pop, jazz, and soul charts in the United States for more than six months.[3]

In 1974, a few weeks after Peggy Lipton gave birth to a baby girl, Kidada, tragedy struck. On a warm August afternoon, Jones was reading in bed when he suddenly felt a pain so fierce that he thought someone had shot him in the head. It was a medical emergency. An aneurysm, a swollen artery, ruptured in his brain and was leaking blood inside his skull at the base of his neck. Jones remembers the intensity of the pain: "I could feel death. I wasn't ready to go, but I could sense in a flash, what it would be like not being here. . . . I just wasn't ready to go."[4]

Jones was lucky. Many people who have a ruptured aneurysm die instantly because their artery gives way like a punctured tire. (It was an aneurysm that killed actor/martial arts artist Bruce Lee.) But Jones's aneurysm was a slow leak, not a blowout. Because it was not deep within the brain, doctors could operate. However, in tests to prepare for the operation, they found another problem—Jones had another aneurysm just about ready to pop on the other side of his brain.

Now the odds were even greater against him because the doctors would have to operate twice. One operation would take place in a few days when his condition stabilized; the other would be several weeks later.

Both operations involved hours of surgery, with doctors drilling through a portion of Jones's scalp and skull, lifting out damaged arteries smaller than strands of spaghetti, putting a metal clip on the arteries, and installing a metal plate to replace the original skull bone. The operation required precise skill. If the doctor's scalpel moved even a millimeter in the wrong direction, Jones could die or become paralyzed, blind, deaf, or even all three—for the rest of his life.

Doctors shaved Jones's head and marked the area to be operated on with permanent ink. He was wheeled into the operating room at Cedars-Sinai Medical Center in Los Angeles, where it took surgeons seven and a half hours to operate.

Although the first operation was an emergency, Jones and Lipton had time to think (eight weeks) before the second one. "I was scared," Jones said about the second operation. "I just knew I wouldn't make it. . . . But . . . I was serious about *not* dying. Hey, man, you want to get back to your old lady and your kids, and so you *fight* to come through."[5]

Less than three months later, surgeons opened up his brain again. This operation was also a success. The experiences of facing death changed Jones's life. He felt he had been given another chance in life. "When I came out of the anesthesia the second time," Jones said, "I wanted to jump out of bed and yell 'Wow! I made it again! I'm still here!' . . . You . . . start looking at everything in a different light."[6]

The operation taught Jones that he needed to take better care of his body. Before the operations, Jones had never exercised a day in his life. Now he began practicing yoga and meditation. There would be other changes in Jones's life as well. Traveling through airports now takes longer for Jones because the metal plates in his head set off the metal detectors. Because of the metal clips in his brain, doctors told him he must never play the trumpet again. The pressure might make the metal clips vibrate off his arteries.

Jones was told by his doctors to take it easy for a while. This time, he obeyed. Christmas 1974 he spent lying in bed and planning his next creative move. "[The operation] taught me to fully follow through in living a minute at a time. It gave me a much broader understanding of what present time is about."[7] The operation also taught Jones that time is precious. Today when he cares for someone, he tells the person—immediately. Jones says that his friends now call him a "hugging machine."[8]

Before the operation, Jones had been a composing machine, exploring new electronic sounds and rhythms. New equipment, like the wahwah pedal for the guitar and piano, and the synthesizer, were opening up new styles for jazz and R&B. After the huge success of the album *Body Heat*, A&M Records was eager to follow up with another album.

In February 1975, his doctors pronounced Jones fully recovered. Jones, however, was a little afraid of jumping into the music world again. With

One year after his brain surgery, Quincy Jones and his wife, actress Peggy Lipton, attended a Hollywood party for musician Ray Charles. Quincy Jones and Ray Charles had been friends since their teen years.

encouragement from his doctors, he decided to go back to work by taking a small group on tour in Japan. He was very weak, but his doctors said it would be all right as long as he did not try to play trumpet. Although it had been years since Jones played the trumpet, it is quite different to be told that you must never play it again. It is the ultimate irony that Jones, the man with the most Grammy Award nominations in history, can never blow a note of music again without its possibly killing him.

In Japan he met two brothers who played with him on that tour. George and Louis Johnson were Los Angeles natives who had been playing bass and guitar since they were teens. The brothers could not read music, but they had talent. Jones liked several of their original tunes. When he planned for his next album, he decided to use the Johnson brothers.

Jones assembled a fifteen-member band and recorded the album *Mellow Madness*. Like *Body Heat*, this new album relied more on rhythm than strings and horns. Some of the tunes on the album included Jones's "Beautiful Black Girl," the Johnson brothers' "Listen (What It Is)," and Stevie Wonder's "My Cherie Amour." Jones dedicated the album to Wonder. Jones called him "the music and poet laureate of our times." Under Jones's guidance, the Johnson brothers recorded their own album, *Look Out For #1*, in 1976.

That same year, Jones and Peggy Lipton had another baby girl, named Rashida.

Although it had been nearly four years since he had written a television or movie score, Jones found himself writing music scores again in 1977. At a party he met Alex Haley, author of *Roots*. Haley wrote this book to tell the story of his family and their passage as slaves from Africa to the United States. When it was made into a television miniseries, Jones was chosen to write the music.

Using African chants and rhythms woven into the music to represent the horrors of slavery, Jones made millions of people aware of African music. The concluding segment of the series captured the third-highest ratings in television history.

For Jones, *Roots* was an opportunity to show the world a style of music that he had loved for years. "African music had always been regarded in the West as primitive and savage," said Jones. "But when you take the time to really study it, you see that it's as structured and sophisticated as European classical music. . . . From gospel, blues, jazz, soul, R&B, rock 'n' roll, all the way to rap, you can trace the roots straight back to Africa."[9] Jones won another Grammy for the *Roots* score.

In 1978, Jones was hired to write the score and be the musical director of *The Wiz*, an African-American version of *The Wizard of Oz*. Although the musical was not a big

Quincy Jones in 1987 with daughters Kidada (on left) and Rashida.

success, it introduced Jones to a twenty-year-old singer named Michael Jackson, who played the part of the Scarecrow in the movie version.

Michael Jackson had begun performing in 1969 in his family's group, the Jackson Five. After signing with the record company Motown, the group was topping the charts, selling millions of albums. By the age of fourteen, Michael Jackson was a millionaire. In 1971, he began making solo albums and switched record labels in 1975 to Epic, a division of CBS.

Working on *The Wiz*, Jones heard the enormous talent in Michael Jackson's voice. He was also impressed with Jackson's self-discipline and the fact that Jackson listened to Jones's suggestions and criticisms. With Jones's ear for producing and Michael Jackson's talent, the two were destined to make record history—and they did.

In 1979, Jones produced Jackson's *Off the Wall* album. Although Jones did little of the arranging himself, he was in charge of the recording sessions. He selected the tunes and picked the musicians. Jones decided the order of the songs to appear on the album, choosing just the right combination of ballads and fast tunes. He decided against overdubs (re-recording in places where there are mistakes), and he judged the final mix (the loudness of high instruments, low instruments, rhythm section, or vocals) on the final cut. Jones knew the album would be a success: When he heard the music in the studio, the hair on his arms stood straight up, a sign that has "never once been wrong," Jones said.[10] Four singles from the album went to number one on the charts, and the album sold 8 million copies—an amazing number in 1979.

As the 1980s began, Jones formed his own record label, Qwest. In 1981, he produced his first single on Qwest, with Patti Austin and James Ingram singing "Baby, Come to Me." The single climbed to number one on the charts. He also won two Grammys in 1981: Producer of the Year for the Qwest album *The Lady and Her Music: Lena Horne*, and Best R&B Performance for the A&M album *The Dude*. Jones produced, conducted, and arranged the music for both albums.

By 1984, the Jones/Jackson team made another album and also a video that was filmed like a movie. However, Jones was apprehensive. Another project would have to be as good as or better than the *Off the Wall* album. After they recorded and mixed the music for the new album, *Thriller*, Jones, Jackson, and the other musicians listened to it one last time before pressing the records.

"That record sounded . . . *terrible*," Jones said. "Michael cried. So, we decided to hell with the deadline, . . . took time off, came back, took one tune a day and brought this baby home. . . . If the record had gone out, it would never have been over, it would have been a *disaster*."[11]

The sound on *Thriller* had been poorly mixed, Jones said, because they were in a rush to complete it. Postponing the deadline was the right thing to do, Jones added. When the album was finally released in 1982, *Thriller*, with the single "Beat It," sold 41 million copies. It became the best-selling album in history. Jackson and Jones won Grammys for Album of the Year and Record of the Year in 1983.

The following year, Jones and Jerry Lubbock wrote the theme for the twenty-third Olympics, held in Los Angeles. The song, named "Grace," became the official gymnastics theme, too. Jones won a Grammy for Best Arrangement of an Instrumental.

With his string of successes, Jones was the natural choice to produce the "We Are the World" relief effort. It held the record for the best-selling single for more than ten years. Then, after these back-to-back successes, Jones turned to yet another creative area— producing movies. It was a natural step from film scorer and record producer to movie producer. Jones selected *The Color Purple*, a novel written by Alice Walker. It struck him as a story that the public should see and hear through film. The story was about two African-American sisters in the rural South who were victims of both racism and sexism.

Jones's enthusiasm convinced a famous director in

Hollywood, Steven Spielberg, to work on the project. Later, Jones would say that he "took a film-making degree from the USS—the University of Steven Spielberg." He added: "In doing a soundtrack, you are only involved after the movie is completed. But this was the first time I had hands-on experience over a full eleven months, from start to finish. It was real hard work and I loved every minute of it."[12]

While casting actors for the movie, Jones discovered a young woman named Oprah Winfrey on local television in Chicago. He decided to cast Winfrey and comedian Whoopi Goldberg in leading roles. Both women won Oscar nominations for their performances.

Jones became a mega-media superstar. But he had to pay a very steep price in his personal life. His twelve-year marriage to Peggy Lipton ended. Lipton, quoted in *People* magazine, said, "Our love never changed but Quincy's life changed after his success. The popularity made demands on his time and his life, and he had to change to meet them."[13]

The media reported that their divorce was an amicable one. Both Lipton and Jones are devoted to their two daughters, Kidada and Rashida. They decided to live close to each other so it would easier for the children to visit. Lipton told the magazine *Redbook* that it was not easy being one of the few interracial couples in the public eye. "But Quincy and I had a lot

Actor Willard Pugh as Harpo and Oprah Winfrey as Sophia in the movie *The Color Purple,* produced by Quincy Jones. On a visit to Chicago, Jones discovered Oprah Winfrey and cast her in his movie. She won an Oscar nomination for her performance.

of love that carried us through," she said. "[I] wasn't going to stop loving Quincy or stop loving my children just because he was black and I was white. . . . I believe that Kidada and Rashida have the best of both worlds."[14]

In the wake of Jones's successes—his Grammys, his Oscar nominations, the "We Are the World" event—were now three failed marriages and six children. Combined with his exhaustion, the divorce weighed heavily on him. The failure of his family life would strike a harsher blow to Jones than any medical condition he had suffered in the past.

8

RAPPING
WITH LIFE

When Jones's marriage to Peggy Lipton collapsed, so did he. Depression set in as he dealt with memory lapses and exhaustion. The doctors told Jones he was suffering from an adrenal gland problem. "But I think that was just kind of a fancy name for nervous breakdown," Jones said. "[They] told me to pull the plug and get away, go straight back to nature."[1]

One of Jones's friends, the actor Marlon Brando, let Jones use his home on an island in the Pacific. It was a perfect retreat. So Jones left his Hollywood world and flew to Tahiti, a place with gentle ocean breezes, lots of sun, and quiet peace.

Alice Walker, the author of *The Color Purple*, gave Jones several spiritual books to read, study, and digest on the island. Among the books he took with him were the Bible, *The Road Less Traveled* by M. Scott Peck, and *The First Rays of Dawn* by Bhola Nath. After his divorce and breakdown, Jones needed to dig inside himself and figure out his life. Reading might help him find answers.

Brando employed a staff of thirteen Tahitians at his home. The Tahitians were very kind to Jones. They devoted themselves to helping him. They ate simply and shared their meals with him. For example, on a walk with Jones, they might reach up for a papaya and cut it open, or break open a coconut for milk. If they were fishing, they all sometimes ate the fish raw, straight from the sea.

They also taught him about their beliefs. They shared with him the stories of the spirits of the ancient Tahitians. They showed Jones a slower and simpler pace to live. Being with them healed Jones. Later he would say that he felt dead during this time—not physically, but spiritually.

After a month in Tahiti, Jones felt whole again. As simple as it sounds, he learned that one of the most important things in the world is a good night's sleep, something that he had often ignored in his hurried past. Jones learned to slow down his pace and live every moment completely. He vowed to spend more time with the most important people in his life—his children. He decided to remain productive musically, but not so productive that he was rushing to get everything finished. "You're not ever going to finish everything you set out to do," he said.[2]

Back home in Los Angeles, he began new musical projects. He produced another album with Michael Jackson, *Bad*. Both Jackson and Jones were nominated for Grammys. Now Jones wanted to produce a record album under his own name. His last record was *The Dude* in 1981. He wanted his new album to be special: to cross musical boundaries and styles and yet bring them together, showing that all music uses the same twelve notes. Along the way, his son, Quincy Jones III, introduced Jones to yet another form of music—hip-hop.

To many adults, hip-hop was nothing more than a barrage of beats, monotone melodies, and vulgar lyrics. In short, hip-hop, or rap, was not music but noise. However, Jones heard and saw something else: He saw rebellious teens who were angry at racial injustices, had contempt for authority, and were singling themselves out with their own ways to dress. Jones saw a parallel between hip-hop and bebop. Beboppers, back in the forties, rebelled against the white, commercial takeover of swing. Hip-hoppers

Quincy Jones and Michael Jackson at the 1984 Grammy Awards ceremony. Jones and Jackson made record history with their album *Thriller*. This album sold 41 million copies, more than any other record in history. A few years later, Jones produced another album, *Bad*, with Jackson.

emerged in the late seventies, rebelling against the white, commercial takeover of black music in the form of disco.

"Rap and bebop are about improvisation, incredible spontaneity and interesting rhythms," he said. "My son is a hip-hop junkie, and I was the same way with bebop. I saw similarities. The spirit is the same, the rebelliousness."[3]

Music is always evolving and changing, Jones says. For years, he had been looking for a way to chronicle the history of African-American music from its roots in West Africa to the music of today. Using both hip-hop and bebop on his album *Back on the Block* was a way for Jones to do just that. Jones also wanted to do an album that would celebrate his place in the music business.

In 1989, he gathered together on one recording the biggest names in jazz: Miles Davis, Sarah Vaughan, Ella Fitzgerald, Al Jarreau, George Benson, James Moody, Bobby McFerrin, Take 6, Herbie Hancock, and a newcomer, twelve-year-old Tevin Campbell. He also brought in rappers: Kool Moe Dee, Big Daddy Kane, Melle Mel, and Ice-T. One tune, "Jazz Corner of the World—Birdland," is a synthesis of rappers telling the history of bebop, mixed with instrumental solos and scatting (jazz singing with nonsense syllables).

Even Jones himself and his son rap together on the opening song, "Back on the Block." The recording engineer, Bruce Swedien, recorded sounds Jones created on his own body and ran them through an enhancer. The sound Jones made by beating on his chest became a drum sound; scratching his head became a shaker. Jones is always trying new ways to be creative in making music. In 1989, the album won Jones another Grammy.

About the same time that Jones was working on the *Back on the Block* album, Warner Brothers was producing a documentary on Jones's life, *Listen Up: The Lives of Quincy Jones*. This 1990 movie is constructed in an unusual, kaleidoscopic way. Instead of moving from one subject to another in chronological order, it is organized more like a jazz piece, with a recurrent theme—Quincy Jones and who he is to each of the people in the movie. Jones talks about his life. So do many stars whose lives he touched, including people who normally do not do interviews, such as Frank Sinatra, Barbra Streisand, and Michael Jackson.

Making the movie brought up some bad memories—memories from his childhood and memories of his later busy life that took time away from his family. Jones's personal life had been a roller coaster of ups and downs, with occasional despair hidden behind gold and platinum records, Oscars, Emmys, and Grammys. Roger Ebert, film critic for the *Chicago Sun-Times*, noted that the film is "not a once-over-lightly PR [public relations] job, but a movie about the peaks and valleys of a man's life."[4] *Listen Up* put all the pieces of Jones's life together for almost two hours on the big screen. Now it was an open book for the entire world.

"Because people have seen me on the scene for so long, they think I was born in Buckingham Palace or something," Jones said at the screening of the movie. "It's been a long time, longer than most of them are old, so they don't put it all together."[5]

With one exception, Jones had not looked back on his five decades of making music until *Listen Up* was filmed. The one exception was after a concert at the Kennedy Center in Washington, D.C., in 1986. "It was one of the heaviest things that happened in my life," he said. Three autograph seekers approached after the show, "and the daughter had 'We Are the World,' the granddaughter had 'Thriller,' and the grandmother had 'Sinatra/Basie.' It blew my mind."[6]

9

Corporate Renaissance Man

I magine creating a show that features hundreds of dancers, musicians, and famous actors and actresses—a show that will be seen by more than one billion pairs of eyes. That's the order for the show of the Academy of Motion Pictures Arts and Sciences that awards golden statuettes known as Oscars for outstanding work in movie production and performance. And the show happens every year.

Producing a show like the Academy Awards is an awesome task. So is producing a Presidential Inaugural Ball—especially an Inaugural Ball that features seven parties going on at once. Quincy Jones has produced both of these major events. Even the President of the United States knew how to dial "Q" for success: President Bill Clinton asked Jones to produce his 1993 Inaugural Ball. A few years later, the Academy Awards people asked Jones to produce their 1996 show.

When Jones produces a musical party, there promises to be all kinds of music: from bebop to hip-hop, big bands to rock 'n' roll. His productions are sleek and dazzling, with heavy doses of pop culture. Whenever Jones puts his creative touch to an entertainment canvas, he creates performance art on a grandiose scale.

"If I do a record or movie, I try to do something nobody else is doing," said Jones, explaining why his shows sparkle with life. "But it has to be dressed up with eye candy and ear candy that make it pop . . . you have to find places where you can put a new fingerprint on it. . . . It has to sizzle."[1]

On the night of March 28, for three and a half hours, the 1996 Academy Awards show *did* sizzle. However, weeks before the ceremony, it seemed there was a possibility that the show might fizzle. The Reverend Jesse Jackson was organizing a protest to call attention to what he called "institutionalized racism" within the motion picture industry. He believed there were not enough minority nominations. Out of 166

Quincy Jones and actor/comedian Eddie Murphy arrive at the Cannes Film Festival in May 1991. At the end of the eighties, Eddie Murphy was America's biggest box-office draw.

nominations for Academy Awards, only one was for a nonwhite person.

Jackson asked those who agreed with his protest to wear a multicolored ribbon. He also wanted them to picket television stations that aired the show around the nation and even the Academy Awards ceremony itself in Hollywood. Television talk-show host Oprah Winfrey was angered by the protest. She pointed out that the 1996 show would be the most multicultural of any because Quincy Jones was producing it. Also, Whoopi Goldberg was going to be the emcee and Winfrey would be interviewing celebrities as they arrived.

On the night of the big show, Jackson's protest faded into the glittery evening. Whoopi Goldberg poked fun at Jackson's request for attendees to wear the ribbons by saying, "You don't ask a black woman to buy an expensive dress and then cover it with ribbons."[2] Jones did wear a ribbon on his tuxedo, but he said that the Academy Awards was not the place for Jackson to protest because the academy does not control hiring in Hollywood. Only a few hundred protesters appeared at some television station offices around the country.

One of the highlights of the Academy Awards show was Goldberg's opening monologue. Another was a moving speech given by actor Christopher Reeve, known to millions of viewers as "Superman," from the movie series. Reeve had been paralyzed a year earlier in a horse-riding accident. His appearance at the Academy Awards was a surprise to the audience. What the audience did not see, however, was what happened behind the scenes. Twenty minutes before he was to speak, Reeve discovered that the orchestra was going to play "Theme From Superman." He did not want the song played, so Jones had to race to the orchestra pit to tell musical director Tom Scott.

With Jones in the captain's seat, the show was one of the grandest that Hollywood had ever seen. Jones admitted later that producing the Academy Awards was really terrifying.[3]

Making entertainment sizzle is Jones's gift to the world. Jones has worked in the business of making music for decades. He has been creative as a musician as well as behind a business desk, behind a mixing board, and standing on a conductor's podium.

Combining his experience as a record company executive, arranger, performer, and producer, Jones had started his own record company, Qwest, in 1980. The chairman of Warner Brothers, Mo Ostin, a good friend of Jones's, financed the company in a fifty-fifty partnership. Today Qwest is still cranking out hit albums. Part of Qwest's success is based on its founder's philosophy that music should not be put into categories. Jones loathes only one category: bad music.

The Reverend Jesse Jackson was one of many guests at a 1995 tribute to Quincy Jones, celebrating his fifty years in the music business in New York. Jones and the Reverend Jackson have worked together on many projects over the years.

Qwest has produced records by such artists as James Ingram, Frank Sinatra, the Winans (a gospel act), R&B vocalist Tevin Campbell, Tamia, jazz musician Milt Jackson, Brazilian musician Dori Caymmi, and veteran entertainer (and Jones's longtime friend) Ray Charles. Qwest has also released movie soundtracks, including *Boyz N the Hood*, *Malcolm X*, and *Sarafina!* Jones expanded Qwest in 1994 to form an offshoot label that deals in promotion, distribution, and marketing. Named Jungle Records, this company is headed by his son, Quincy Jones III. One of his daughters, Jolie Jones-Levine, is the director of A&R for Qwest.

Part of Jones's motivation to invest in these multimedia companies is to find a way to pull his children into his life. "All my kids are talented," he says. The companies have the "capacity to encompass anything they may want to do, to learn, to grow. And, we're finally going to have a chance to be with each other a lot, because the ultimate goal is not just to love each other and be around each other, but to create together."[4]

Jones, in building a media empire, was not content with just the spoken or sung word. In 1992, he ventured into the written word by publishing a magazine. Jones, David Salzman, and Time Inc. Ventures launched *Vibe*, a journal of black urban culture. Jones envisioned a magazine like *Rolling Stone*, to promote hip-hop. Jones believes hip-hop is a state of mind. "It's a lifestyle of different people left out of the mainstream who started their own culture," he said. "People who have their own slang, mannerisms, dance, graphic arts.[5]

"Hip-hop is about today, it's about what's happening right now before us," he said. "It is not negative, as a lot of people seem to think."[6] With hip-hop culture, Jones saw a way both to expand his business empire and to help along the trend toward African Americans' owning their art. "There's never been a [mainstream] magazine where black writers can come and have a home," he said. "We didn't really have a place to go."[7]

Vibe, with a circulation that had grown to 450,000 by 1996, focuses on black culture through features on fashions, music, and television. In addition, in 1997 Jones launched *Vibe*, a late-night talk show patterned after *Vibe* magazine.

Jones lives his life to the fullest each day. In 1993, he became a father again, when actress Nastassja Kinski gave birth to a girl, Kenya, his seventh child. That same year, he signed a joint partnership deal with Time-Warner Enterprises and another business partner, David Salzman, to form QDE. Jones is the chairman of QDE. Salzman, who was the executive producer for television's *Mike Douglas Show*, as well as the former president of Lorimar Telepictures, has experience producing shows ranging from live concerts to documentaries.

QDE produces television shows, movies, and videos. Some of its television projects include *Fresh Prince of Bel Air, Mad TV,* the *Jenny Jones Show, In the House* (starring rapper L. L. Cool J), and *Mr. Rudy. Fresh Prince of Bel Air* ran for six consecutive seasons on NBC and is now in syndication.

Originally, the idea for *Fresh Prince* had been turned down by two other television companies. The show's idea was based on the life of Benny Medina, a Warner Brothers Records executive. After he was turned down by other companies, he approached Jones with the story. Jones then presented the idea to NBC. Ten weeks later, *Fresh Prince* made its debut and soon became a top-rated program. Jones has a gift for knowing what the public will like.

QDE has plans for other shows and movies: *Don Quixote; The Pulse,* about an urban superhero; *Hoover,* about the former FBI chief; a remake of *A Star Is Born;* two features using *Mad* magazine characters Alfred E. Neuman and the spies of *Spy vs. Spy;* and a drama about a black female police officer, *The Jacklean Davis Story.*

Jones did not want to just create the shows. He wanted to broadcast them as well. In 1994, he teamed up with several businessmen, including Hall of Fame football player Willie Davis, television producer Don

Cornelius, and television journalist Geraldo Rivera, to form Qwest Broadcasting. The company's first purchases were WATL-TV in Atlanta and WNOL-TV in New Orleans. It is now one of the largest minority-owned broadcasting companies in the United States.[8]

Jones is connected to all forms of pop culture—television, music, movies, and magazines. A natural extension of combining all of these media is computer technology. In 1994, Jones and Salzman teamed up with a Dallas-based company, 7th Level, to form QD7. The company was created to blend filmmaking with computer animation to produce interactive multimedia CD-ROMs. The idea of a CD-ROM fascinated Jones, who had been looking for a way to illustrate how music has evolved. Originally, he planned to produce a television documentary, but a CD-ROM was the perfect vehicle for the project because users could interact with the information.

Jones's research into the roots of music began back in 1970, a few years before he wrote the score to *Roots*. Back then, he was wondering about the African connection to pop music. Whether the music is hip-hop, bebop, or whatever-bop, Jones says that it all comes from the same source: Africa. "Rappers want to go off in their own little cubbyhole, jazz over here, blues over there, but when it gets down to it, they're all related," he says. "Family. It all comes from Africa. And the spirit, the strength of it, comes from church."[9]

Jones's CD-ROM is called *Q's Jook Joint*, a combination of videos, music, documentaries, interviews, and animation all in one package. It explores not only music's roots but also how social and political contexts are woven into the music. "We're using 'jook joint' (as in juke joint) as a metaphor, because those were the only places back in the '20s and '30s where black people could go to dance, talk and move up in the musical world," Jones said. "Juke joints were places where people like Louis Armstrong and Bessie Smith could perfect their craft."[10]

"It's a fascinating passage through history," Jones said about researching the evolution of music. "You can really see the interconnectedness of things, and the cross-pollination that occurred and is still occurring today."[11] For example, Jones noticed that when he was at the inauguration of President Nelson Mandela of South Africa, there was a praise shouter who introduced Mandela to the audience. "That was the same as a rapper," Jones said. "Rappers of today have very strong roots, whether they know it or not."[12]

The past is as important as the future to Jones. People have to see where they have been to know where they are going, he says. Combining his past with the future is Jones's album with the same name as the CD-ROM—*Q's Jook Joint*. Jones says it "bridges the gap between the younger and older generations. You have Ray Charles and Brandy singing ["Stuff Like That"].

Quincy Jones shares a joke and a kiss with talk-show host Oprah Winfrey at the 1995 Academy Awards.

She wasn't even born when some of these songs were originally recorded."[13] The album evolved into a kind of musical survey of the past fifty years of the music Jones lived with. It is a Jones brew of jazz, hip-hop, pop, funk, and R&B.

Jones is still adding hyphens to his name: musician-composer-arranger-producer-educator-executive in the record, television, and film industries. As for new media, he says: "Everything still boils down to a song and a story, and I don't care what carriage it's on. It still boils down to a song and a story."[14]

In 1995, Jones was awarded the Jean Hersholdt Humanitarian Award by the Academy of Motion Picture Arts and Sciences. The award is given to an individual in the motion picture field whose humanitarian efforts have brought credit to the industry.

Jones was donating his energies to helping others long before the "We Are the World" fund-raising event. In 1973, he helped form IBAM (Institute for Black-American Music) and Operation Breadbasket. He has worked for black EXPO, an annual event sponsored by black business communities. In 1990, he launched the Listen Up Foundation, a nonprofit task force to combat drugs, illiteracy, violence, and poverty among inner-city youth. When Jones accepted the Hersholdt award, he proclaimed his belief that barriers of all kinds can be broken down in both music and life—with love. No one, not even Jones, could have predicted where his future would take him when he was eight years old and living in the ghetto of Chicago's South Side. He had dreams that he would not let die. He believed in himself.

"You've got to dream real big," he said. "But . . . don't just say, 'Oh God, I wish I was happy,' . . . you've got to be very specific or it won't happen."[15]

That belief has taken him far: nominated for an unprecedented seventy-seven Grammys, winning twenty-six; and honored with numerous Emmy and Oscar nominations. He helped create the best-selling record in history, Michael Jackson's *Thriller*, and he has written dozens of movie scores and television themes.

The list of his accomplishments is long, but they did not come easily: two aneurysms, a nervous breakdown, three failed marriages, and seven children that he wishes he had spent more time with. For all the pain and joy that life has handed him, he has never stopped reaching for his goals. Yes, he has made mistakes, he says, but those difficult lessons have taught him a deeper understanding of life.

"Learn from [mistakes]," he advises others. "Grow from them. And teach your pain to *sing*. . . . All I can say is, after living through the pain and sorrows in my own life, if that's the price I've had to pay for all the joy I've known, it's been worth every minute of it, man."[16]

The universal quality that Jones sees in himself and other successful musicians is that they have a God-given talent and, he says, "an obligation to develop, nurture and build it."[17] That obligation is why Jones has worked hard all his life. His dream has always been to be known as a good musician. "I've always gone for the music that gives me goose bumps, music that touches my heart and soul," he adds.[18]

Touching the world's heart and soul is what Quincy Delight Jones, Jr., does best.

CHRONOLOGY

1933—Born Quincy Delight Jones, Jr., in Chicago, Illinois, on March 14.

1943—Family moves to Bremerton, Washington.

1947—Begins studying trumpet; first gig at a YMCA dance; soon meets friend Ray Charles.

1951—Accepts scholarship to Schillinger House in Boston; leaves Schillinger House for road gig with the Lionel Hampton Big Band; tours United States and Europe; records first big-band composition, "Kingfish."

1953—Leaves Lionel Hampton's band and moves to New York City.

1953—Records various arrangements and composi-
-1956   tions; plays trumpet; producer for various musical artists.

1956—Becomes musical director for Dizzy Gillespie's sixteen-piece band on the "World Statesmen Tour" of Europe, the Middle East, and South America.

1957—Relocates to Paris, France; studies composition with Nadia Boulanger.

1959—Becomes musical director for Harold Arlen's blues opera, *Free and Easy*, set to tour Europe with an all-star big band, but show closes and band stays in Europe.

1961—Becomes music director for Mercury Records in New York City.

1963—Discovers Leslie Gore and produces his first number-one single, "It's My Party"; scores his first Hollywood film, *The Pawnbroker* (1965).

1964—Wins his first Grammy for arrangement of "I Can't Stop Loving You" for Count Basie Orchestra; becomes vice president at Mercury Records.

1965—Travels nationwide as conductor for Frank Sinatra and Count Basie; moves to Hollywood.

1967—Scores themes for television's *Ironside* and for two movies, *In the Heat of the Night* and *In Cold Blood*.

1974—Has two brain operations for aneurysms.

1977—Scores *Roots*.

1978—Scores *The Wiz*; meets Michael Jackson.

1979—Makes album *Off the Wall* with Michael Jackson.

1980—Forms record company Qwest Records.

1982—Records album *Thriller* with Michael Jackson; wins 1983 Grammy Awards for Album of the Year and Record of the Year, and Grammy nomination for Best R&B Instrumental Performance of song "Billie Jean."

1985—Co-produces *The Color Purple*; discovers Oprah Winfrey; produces "We Are the World," raising more than $50 million for famine relief.

1990—Wins Grammy's Legends Award (most nominated artist in Grammy's history with 77 nominations and 26 wins); forms Quincy

Jones Entertainment Company, a multimedia entertainment company; produces *The Fresh Prince of Bel Air*.

1992—Founds the magazine *Vibe*.

1993—Produces the Presidential Inauguration Ball; forms QDE, a production company.

1994—Forms Qwest Broadcasting Company, one of the largest minority-owned broadcast companies in the United States.

1995—Receives the Jean Hersholdt Humanitarian Award from the Academy of Motion Picture Arts and Sciences; releases album *Q's Jook Joint*.

1996—Executive producer for 1996 Academy Awards ceremony; wins Lifetime Achievement Award from the Thelonius Monk Institute; researches and produces CD-ROM *Q's Jook Joint*.

1997—Launches late-night talk show *Vibe*.

Music by
Quincy Jones

Selected Discography

Quincy Jones Swedish-American All Stars.
(Metronome, 1953)

This Is How I Feel About Jazz: Quincy Jones All Stars.
(ABC-Paramount, 1956)

Birth of a Band: Quincy Jones and His Orchestra.
(Mercury, 1959)

The Great Wide World of Quincy Jones: Quincy Jones and His Orchestra. (Mercury, 1959)

Around the World: Quincy Jones and His Orchestra.
(Mercury, 1961)

The Quintessence: Quincy Jones and His Orchestra.
(Mercury, 1962)

It Might As Well Be Swing: Frank Sinatra with Count Basie and His Orchestra. (Reprise, 1964)

Sinatra at the Sands with Count Basie & the Orchestra.
(Reprise, 1966)

Walking in Space: Quincy Jones and His Orchestra.
(A&M, 1969)

Smackwater Jack: Quincy Jones and His Orchestra.
(A&M, 1971)

Body Heat: Quincy Jones and His Orchestra.
(A&M, 1974)

Sounds . . . and Stuff Like That! Quincy Jones and His Orchestra. (A&M, 1978)

The Dude: Quincy Jones and His Orchestra. (A&M, 1982)

Thriller: Michael Jackson with Quincy Jones Orchestra. (Epic, 1982)

L.A. Is My Lady: Frank Sinatra with Quincy Jones Orchestra. (Qwest, 1984)

We Are the World. (Polygram, 1985)

Back on the Block: Quincy Jones. (Qwest, 1989)

Miles & Quincy Live at Montreux. (Warner Brothers Records, 1993)

Q's Jook Joint. (Qwest, 1995)

Selected Movie Scores

The Boy in the Tree (Sweden, 1964)

The Pawnbroker (1965)

The Slender Thread (1965)

Mirage (1966)

Walk, Don't Run (1966)

In the Heat of the Night (1967)

In Cold Blood (1967)

Enter Laughing (1967)

The Deadly Affair (1967)

The Split (1968)

For Love of Ivy (1968)

The Lost Man (1969)

John and Mary (1969)

The Italian Job (1969)

Cactus Flower (1969)

Bob & Carol & Ted & Alice (1969)

Last of the Mobile Hot Shots (1970)

They Call Me Mr. Tibbs! (1970)

The Out-of-Towners (1970)

Brother John (1970)

The Hot Rock (1971)

The Anderson Tapes (1971)

Dollars (1971)

The New Centurions (1972)

The Getaway (1972)

The Wiz (1978)

The Color Purple (1985)

Listen Up: The Lives of Quincy Jones (1990)

Selected Television Credits

Ironside—scored the pilot and eight episodes (1967)

Split Second to an Epitaph—wrote theme for TV movie (1969)

The Bill Cosby Show—scored 56 episodes (1969)

The NBC Mystery Movie—wrote theme (1971)

The New Bill Cosby Show—wrote theme (1972)

Killer by Night—wrote theme for TV movie (1972)

Sanford and Son—wrote theme (1972)

Roots—scored miniseries (1977)

In the Heat of the Night—wrote theme (1988)

The Jesse Jackson Show—executive producer (1990)

Fresh Prince of Bel Air—executive producer (1990)

An American Reunion—executive producer (Presidential Inauguration/HBO) (1993)

The Return of Ironside—wrote theme for TV movie (1993)

Nashville Salutes the Ryman—executive producer (CBS TV special) (1994)

Kennedy Center Presents: The Concert of the Americas—executive producer (PBS special) (1995)

Mad TV—executive producer (1995)

In the House—executive producer (1996)

Vibe—executive producer (1997)

CHAPTER NOTES

Chapter 1
1. Courtney Sale Ross, *Listen Up: The Lives of Quincy Jones* (New York: Warner Books, 1990), p. 150.
2. Robert Hilburn, "We Are the World," *Billboard*, April 6, 1985, p. USA-34.
3. Ibid., p. USA-10.
4. Ibid., p. USA-3.
5. Gene Seymore, "Quincy Jones, Humanitarian," *New York Newsday*, March 14, 1995, p. B3.
6. Hilburn, p. USA-4.
7. Ibid.
8. Diane Shah, "On Q: For 40 years, Quincy Jones Has Been Where the Music Is," *The New York Times Magazine*, November 18, 1990, p. 60.
9. James T. Jones, "Quincy Jones: The Year of the Q," *JazzTimes*, December 1990, p. 43.
10. Alex Haley, "Quincy Jones," *Playboy*, July 1990, p. 166.

Chapter 2
1. Alex Haley, "Quincy Jones," *Playboy*, July 1990, p. 58.
2. Roger Ebert, "Listen-Up: The Lives of Quincy Jones," *Chicago Sun-Times*, October 5, 1990.
3. Steve Dougherty, "Quincy Jones," *People*, October 15, 1990, p.109.
4. Haley, p. 58.
5. Paul de Barros, *Jackson Street After Hours* (Seattle: Sasquatch Books, 1993), p. 101.
6. Raymond Horricks, *Quincy Jones* (Tunbridge Wells, Kent: Spellmount, 1985), p. 12.
7. de Barros, p. 102.

8. Ibid., p. 105.

9. Lee Underwood, "Q Lives," *Downbeat*, October 23, 1975, p. 14.

10. de Barros, p. 109.

11. Haley, p. 59.

12. Dougherty, p. 109.

13. Haley, p. 59.

Chapter 3

1. Paul de Barros, *Jackson Street After Hours* (Seattle: Sasquatch Books, 1993), p. 107.

2. Ross Russell, *Bird Lives! The High Life and Hard Times of Charlie "Yardbird" Parker* (London: Quartet Books, 1980), p. 358.

3. "History of Rock 'n' Roll: Quincy Jones Interview." On the Internet at http://www.music.warnerbros.com/rocknroll/cmp/quincy.html

Chapter 4

1. Raymond Horricks, *Quincy Jones* (Tunbridge Wells, Kent: Spellmount, 1985), pp. 43–44.

2. Ibid., p. 34.

3. Dizzy Gillespie, with Al Fraser, *To BE, or Not . . . to BOP* (New York: Doubleday, 1979), p. 424.

4. Ibid.

5. Linda Dahl, *Stormy Weather: The Music and Lives of a Century of Jazzwomen* (New York: Pantheon Press, 1984), p. 250.

6. Courtney Sale Ross, *Listen Up: The Lives of Quincy Jones* (New York: Warner Books, 1990), p. 96.

7. Ibid, p. 81.

Chapter 5

1. Lee Underwood, "Q Lives," *Downbeat*, October 23, 1975, p. 14.

2. Ibid.

3. Dafydd Rees and Luke Crampton, *The Encyclopedia of Rock Stars* (New York: DK Publishing, 1996), p. 363.

4. Steve Dougherty, "Quincy Jones," *People*, October 15, 1990, pp. 109–110.

5. Courtney Sale Ross, *Listen Up: The Lives of Quincy Jones* (New York: Warner Books, 1990), p. 105.

6. Ibid., p. 111.

Chapter 6

1. Alex Haley, "Quincy Jones," *Playboy*, July 1990, p. 62.

2. "Q's Jook Joint On-Line." On the Internet at http://www.wbr.com/quincyjones/soundtrack.html

3. Raymond Horricks, *Quincy Jones* (Tunbridge Wells, Kent: Spellmount, 1985), p. 66.

4. Steve Dougherty, "Quincy Jones," *People*, October 15, 1990, p. 110.

5. Diane Shah, "On Q: For 40 years, Quincy Jones Has Been Where the Music Is," *The New York Times Magazine*, November 18, 1990, p. 64.

Chapter 7

1. Raymond Horricks, *Quincy Jones* (Turnbridge Wells, Kent: Spellmount LTD, 1985) p. 77.

2. Joe C. Farr III, "Quincy Jones Page." On the Internet at http://www.duke.edu./%7Ejcf3/

3. Ibid.

4. Charles L. Sanders, "Quincy Jones Talks About Life and Death," *Ebony*, March 1976, p. 133.

5. Ibid., p. 135.

6. Ibid.

7. Aldore Collier, "Quincy Jones Finds Peace," *Ebony*, April 1990, p. 82.

8. Ibid.

9. Courtney Sale Ross, *Listen Up: The Lives of Quincy Jones* (New York: Warner Books, 1990), p. 133.

10. Alex Haley, "Quincy Jones," *Playboy*, July 1990, p. 63.

11. Zan Stewart, "The Quincy Jones Interview," *Downbeat*, April 1985, p. 49.

12. "Q's Jook Joint On-Line." On the Internet at http://www.wbr.com/quincyjones/soundtrack.html

13. David Hutchings, "Peggy Lipton," *People*, April 4, 1988, p. 62.

14. Glenn Esterly, "Peggy Lipton: My Life Is Starting Over," *Redbook*, October 1990, p. 62.

Chapter 8

1. Alex Haley, "Quincy Jones," *Playboy*, July 1990, p. 65.

2. Ibid., p. 66.

3. James T. Jones, "Quincy Jones: The Year of the Q," *Jazz Times*, December 1990, p. 52.

4. Roger Ebert, "Listen-Up: The Lives of Quincy Jones," *Chicago Sun-Times*, October 5, 1990.

5. Richard Harrington, "Quincy Jones: Putting It All Together," *Washington Post*, October 6, 1990, p. C1.

6. Ibid.

Chapter 9

1. Daniel Howard Cerone, "It's Their Party," *TV Guide*, March 23, 1996, p. 25.

2. Laura Smith, "Invisible Ribbons," *PEOPLE Daily Online*, March 27, 1996. On the Internet at http://pathfinder. com/people/daily/96back/960327.html

3. Ken Tucker, "The Show: Great Taste, Still Thrilling," *Entertainment Weekly*, April 5, 1996, p. 32.

4. Richard Harrington, "Quincy Jones: Putting It All Together," *Washington Post*, October 6, 1990, p. C5.

5. Hugh Wyatt, "Quincy's Venture Vibe Is Hip-hoppin' Off the Presses," *New York Daily News*, September 16, 1992, Entertainment Section, p. 1.

6. Ibid.

7. Bruce Newman, "A Cosmic Q Rating," *Los Angeles Times*, November 5, 1995. p. 92.

8. Carolyn Brown, "The Master of Trades," *Black Enterprise*, June 1, 1996, p. 245–246.

9. Sonia Murray, "Jones Retrieves Familiar Vibe on Star-Studded New Release," *Atlanta Constitution*, October 22, 1995, p. L10.

10. Laura Evenson, "Another Door Opens for Quincy Jones: Music Maven Moves Into Multimedia," *San Francisco Chronicle*, June 18, 1995, p. 26.

11. Marilyn A. Gillen, "Quincy's CD-ROM Explores Music's Roots," *Billboard*, May 20, 1995, p. 56.

12. Mark Rowland, "Quincy Jones: A Half Century of Music," *Billboard*, December 16, 1995, p. 26.

13. Brown, p. 244.

14. Evenson, p. 27.

15. Rowland, p. 28.

16. Alex Haley, "Quincy Jones: A Half Century of Music," *Playboy*, July 1990, p. 166.

17. Mark Small, "The Best Is Yet to Come," *Berklee Today*, Spring 1995, p. 16.

18. Wyatt, p. 39.

FURTHER READING

Brown, Carolyn. "The Master of Trades." *Black Enterprise*, June 1996, pp. 244–254.

de Barros, Paul. *Jackson Street After Hours*. Seattle: Sasquatch Books, 1993.

Dougherty, Steve. "Quincy Jones." *People*, October 15, 1990, pp. 103–110.

Horricks, Raymond. *Quincy Jones*. Tunbridge Wells, Kent: Spellmount, 1985.

Jones, Quincy. "50 Years of Black Music." *Ebony*, November 1995, pp. 178–184.

Ross, Courtney Sale. *Listen Up: The Lives of Quincy Jones*. New York: Warner Books, 1990.

Rowland, Mark. "Quincy Jones: A Half Century of Music." *Billboard*, December 16, 1995, pp. 22–50.

Shah, Diane. "On Q: For 40 Years, Quincy Jones Has Been Where the Music Is." *The New York Times Magazine*, November 18, 1990, p. 41.

Internet Sites

Quincy Jones Page http://www.duke.edu./%7Ejcf3/

Quincy Jones ...... http://www.wbr.com/quincyjones/

Vibe magazine site ...... http://www.vibe.com

INDEX